Minding Your Business Manners

Minding Your Business Manners

*Etiquette Tips for Presenting Yourself
Professionally in Every Business Situation*

Marjorie Brody

Barbara Pachter

SkillPath Publications
Mission, KS

Editor: Kelly Scanlon

Page Layout: Rod Hankins and Premila Malik Borchardt

Cover Design: Rod Hankins

Library of Congress Card Catalog Number: 95-71779

ISBN: 1-57294-014-X

10   9   8   7   6   5   4   3   99   00

Printed in the United States of America

Contents

u

Introduction

Competition in today's streamlined, down-sized, re-engineered business world is becoming increasingly fierce. In this competitive atmosphere, it's becoming increasingly likely that factors other than expertise will influence your success. You can't count on technical skill alone to take you to the top.

But, happily, one of the most important of those factors is something so basic you've known it since you were a child. That key to success is good manners—being polite, knowing how to get along with others, making them feel comfortable and important. That's right. It's that simple.

But, if good manners are so simple—and so important—then why are they so often overlooked? Because sometimes we're just too busy. Who has time to remember "little" things like manners? And who cares?

You should care because it's often the "little" things—the small courtesies, subtle niceties, respectful gestures—that clinch the sale, provide the foundation for a relationship, and establish a credible professional image. On the other hand, countless sales, jobs, and other opportunities have been lost as a result of lack of attention to these "little" things.

How are your "company manners"? The following list of the ten most common etiquette errors people make in the workplace will help you evaluate them. Be honest with yourself as you read them.

The Ten Most Common Workplace Etiquette Errors

1. **Speaking before thinking.** Listen to yourself. Do you call people by inappropriate nicknames or other forms of address such as "Hon" or "Babe" that could be interpreted as demeaning or insulting? Do you use vulgar or tasteless humor? Do you insult, criticize, or otherwise embarrass people? Do you spread gossip or rumors?

2. **Wasting other people's time.** Are you frequently late or unprepared for appointments? Do you miss deadlines for turning in assignments? Do you feel that barging into another person's office or interrupting a meeting any time you feel like it is acceptable?

3. **Dressing unprofessionally; sloppy grooming.** Are your clothes too tight, too short, revealing, unkempt? Look in the mirror. Is this the image you want others to judge you by? Is this the image your company wants to project?

4. **Misusing/abusing technology.** Do you tie up other people's fax machines and waste their paper with pages of unsolicited materials? Is it obvious that you use your answering machine to screen unwanted calls? Does your beeper frequently go off in the middle of meetings, even when there's no emergency?

5. **Showing poor telephone manners.** Do you keep people on "hold" too long, neglect to return calls in a timely manner, forget to give messages? Do you confuse people by not identifying yourself properly? Do you eat during phone conversations or slam down the receiver when you're finished talking?

6. **Greeting people improperly—or not at all.** How's your handshake? Is it as limp as a wet noodle—or do you squeeze like a vise? Do you know when a handshake is appropriate? When you're visiting another country, do you just assume that a handshake is the proper greeting?

7. **Practicing poor conversational skills.** Do you interrupt when others are speaking? If you ask a question, do you go on to another subject before the other person can answer? Do your eyes—and your attention—wander when someone else is speaking?

8. **Invading other people's privacy and abusing shared space.** When you're in someone else's office, do you read the papers on his or her desk? Do you eavesdrop on telephone conversations? After using a shared office or conference room, do you forget to clean up after yourself? If you use the last of the paper in the copy machine, do you leave the empty tray for the next person to fill?

9. **Letting poor body language undermine your words.** Do you show a lack of confidence by slouching? Closed-mindedness by crossing your arms? Disinterest by averting your eyes? Your body language speaks louder and more eloquently than anything you say.

10. **Forgetting—or never learning—table manners.** Does a formal table setting intimidate you? Do people comment on your picky eating habits? Do you play "tug of war" with the bill?

Did you recognize yourself in any of these etiquette blunders? Not to worry. You can begin right now to develop the business etiquette skills you need to get ahead—both personally and professionally.

1

Greetings and Introductions

You've no doubt heard that first
meetings make a lasting
impression. It's true. A positive first
encounter can provide a solid
foundation for a positive
relationship. If, however, that first
impression is negative, it could
become an obstacle that you'll
have to work hard to overcome.

6

The Handshake

In the United States, the most common and proper business greeting is the handshake. Many people believe that the way a person shakes hands tells a great deal about his or her personality and competence. For example, a limp handshake can often be interpreted as a sign of weakness or a lack of confidence, while a "death grip" handshake is often considered a sign of aggression and overconfidence.

It's really easy to perfect the professional handshake if you remember these three steps:

1. **Say your name and extend your hand.** Traditionally, the higher ranking person initiates the handshake by extending the hand first. However, if that person doesn't, go ahead and extend your hand. Because it used to be considered proper etiquette for a man to wait for a woman to extend her hand, some men continue to be hesitant about initiating a handshake with a woman. If there is any hesitation on the part of the man, the woman can simplify matters by extending her hand first.

2. **Extend your hand at a slight angle, touch thumb joint to thumb joint, and then wrap your fingers firmly—without cutting off the circulation or breaking any bones—around the other person's palm.** It's all one smooth movement once you get the hang of it.

3. **Pump two or three times.** Then let go and drop your hand.

Knowing *how* to shake hands is the first step. But knowing *when* a handshake is appropriate is just as important. Here are the occasions when it's considered proper etiquette to shake hands:

- During introductions or farewells, whether in one-on-one or group situations

- When greeting someone from outside the company (e.g., a client, customer, vendor, or other visitor)

- When you run into a business acquaintance you haven't seen in a long time

- When you formalize an agreement

- Whenever your good sense tells you to do so

Self-Introduction

An important and exciting part of business life is meeting new people. Of course, it's always more comfortable when there's someone around to make the introductions. Unfortunately, that's not always the case.

When no one is available to introduce you—or when the person you're with forgets to do the honors—it's always good manners to introduce yourself. It's also easier than you might think, if you're prepared.

Take a few minutes to prepare a general self-introduction. It should be brief, informative, and positive, sort of like a ten-second commercial. For example: "Hello, I'm Mary Jones. I'm manager of accounting for XYZ Corporation." Tailor your introduction to the situation. If everyone knows you're from XYZ Corporation, you don't have to announce it.

Practice your introduction out loud in front of a mirror until you feel comfortable with it. Remember to hold your head up, make eye contact, shake hands, and smile.

*I*ntroducing Others

Have you ever been with a group of people to whom you haven't been introduced? Did you feel uncomfortable, left out, even invisible? Some people aren't confident or assertive enough to introduce themselves to people they don't know. In a meeting situation, the "outsider" can be distracted from the business at hand while trying to figure out who's who. That's where you can step in and show your good manners—and professional polish.

Making introductions can be as simple as A-B-C:

A = Authority. Mention the name of the person of greatest authority or importance first. Gender or age is not always the deciding factor. If a client is involved, he or she should be first.

B = Basic. Keep it short and sweet. Say each person's name only one time, unless you give information about the person.

C = Clarify. Give a bit of information about each person. For example: "Mr. Grady, I'd like you to meet Ms. Evans, who is head of marketing for our company. Mr. Grady is vice president of Client Company."

The Give and Take of Business Cards

In some countries, the exchange of business cards is governed by time-honored rituals. But in the United States, the timing and circumstances of presenting cards is not quite as formal.

Traditionally, business card exchanges in this country take place at either the beginning or the end of the first encounter. If you want to offer your card, ask for the other person's card first. In most cases, the other person will then ask for your card. If not, offer one of yours.

Like the old-fashioned calling card, you can use your business card to announce your presence by giving it to the receptionist. This is also polite because it makes it easier for the person at the desk to remember your name and company when informing your host of your arrival.

At meetings, cards are often exchanged prior to the beginning of business to allow everyone to keep the participants' names and areas of expertise or responsibility straight. Discretely referring to a card is much more polite than losing track of the proceedings as you wrack your brain trying to remember the name of the person sitting at the other side of the table.

Your card can also represent you when you aren't physically present. For example, you can enclose your card when forwarding materials to someone or sending a letter to someone you'd like to do business with in the future.

There are times and places when handing out business cards is not proper etiquette. For example, it is not appropriate to distribute cards during a meal. If you want to initiate a card exchange, wait until everyone is finished eating. If you're at a private dinner party, you may carry your cards with you, but don't pass any out unless someone specifically asks you for one.

In any situation and under any circumstances, a good guideline is to be selective in your distribution of business cards. Don't just work your way around the room passing out cards at random. That's not just wasteful—it's obnoxious.

Before giving out your card, think about whether the person might actually have the need or desire to contact you in the future. If the answer is even a possible "yes," by all means, offer your card.

Above all, make sure your business cards fit your professional image. They should be well-designed and printed on high-quality paper. They should also be free of wrinkles, smudges, and tattered edges.

Keep your cards readily available. Carrying cards in a set location in an easily accessible suit or jacket pocket, briefcase, or purse will ensure that they'll always be within easy reach.

*O*pening Lines

The curtain has gone up and the spotlight is on you. No, it's not opening night on Broadway. But it can feel like it when you have to start a conversation with someone you haven't met before.

Initiating small talk is not a science. But it is an art, an important art that can help you overcome the awkwardness of first meetings and connect with people.

Be direct and sincere. Don't try to be cute or funny. You don't know the other person and your humor might be lost or misinterpreted. Here are some polite and proven ways to effectively open up a conversation:

- **Make an upbeat observation.** "This is a very interesting seminar. I've already picked up a lot of valuable information."

- **Ask an open-ended question.** "Where are you from?"

- **Offer a pleasant self-revelation.** "This is my first time in Philadelphia."

If your first opening line fails to draw a response, try another. The open-ended question should work even if the person is shy. If there is still no response, move on. The last thing you want to do is annoy someone.

*T*alking to Anyone About Anything

In some instances, silence is golden. But not when you're trying to get to know someone. Then, it's just plain awkward.

A little small talk can help you bridge the gap between initial introduction and comfortable conversation. It can put people at ease and establish a rapport that can be the foundation for a solid relationship. (See Chapter 3, "Networking," for suggested opening lines.)

One of the best things about small talk is that it's an art you can practice just about anywhere and anytime. You could be passing a co-worker in the hallway, waiting for an elevator with a supervisor, or arriving at a meeting with a prospective client or customer. It takes only a minute or two to make a connection.

Since you never know when the opportunity to initiate small talk will arise, you should always be prepared with a repertoire of ideas and topics. Some always-appropriate conversation openers include the weather, traffic conditions, sports, or, if you're away from your own office, some favorable comment about the city you're visiting or the event you're attending.

Stay away from such conversational taboos as religion, income, anything highly controversial, or any intimate details about your life. Health talk is another no-no—whether it's yours or the other person's.

You can also add to your file of small-talk starters by keeping up with current events. Read your daily newspaper and a few magazines a month. Read your professional journals too. If you happen to be in another city, don't forget to read the local paper. And always keep your eyes open. Knowing what's going on around you can help you to join in any conversation. However, be careful to keep your comments neutral and positive, especially on subjects that can become inflammatory or if you are a guest in someone else's city or country.

Listen when others speak. Besides being the polite thing to do, it can help you learn a great deal about the other person and give you valuable clues about the best way to guide the conversation.

2

Professional Presence

People use a variety of signals to communicate with one another. These signals can be categorized into three major groups: visual, vocal, and verbal. Through these signals we communicate not only what we want and what we think, but who we are as well. The image people form of us as a result is our professional presence.

First impressions are often made within the first five seconds that you meet someone. That doesn't leave a lot of time for catching vocal or verbal cues. However, there are a few vocal signals that can ruin your image in no time. In general, speak slowly enough to be understood and enunciate your words. Act enthused, but not to the extent you appear unprofessional. Similarly, watch your verbal manners. Avoid jargon, buzzwords, and sarcasm. Make certain your humor is appropriate. And don't curse.

The visual signals you send can be even stronger than your vocal and verbal ones. Research shows that 55 percent of the overall impression you make is based solely on visual cues, the things people can see when they look at you. This includes your grooming, dress, gestures, facial expressions, and even the way you stand and carry yourself. The rest of the impression is based on the way you use your voice (vocal) and the words you choose (verbal). Vocal aspects account for 38 percent of your overall image; verbal ones account for only 7 percent.

Obviously, appearance has a lot to do with whether people perceive you favorably. But that doesn't mean you have to look like a movie star to be successful. It only means you have to look, dress, and act like the professional you are.

*B*ody Language

A key component of your visual image is your body language. No matter what words you use to express yourself, your posture, body position, gestures, and facial expressions can either emphasize or seriously undermine your message.

- **Posture.** Standing straight makes you feel more alert and look more confident. Slouching can make you look tired, sloppy, or apathetic. You might also give the impression that you're trying to hide. Keep in mind that good posture is just as important when you're sitting.

- **Movement.** Keep your movements simple and naturally graceful. Hesitant movements make you appear timid or unsure.

- **Gestures.** Use varied, natural gestures to reinforce your verbal message. Don't be overly dramatic. Hands on hips, pounding fists, and crossed arms tend to make people feel uncomfortable. Finger-pointing can make people feel defensive. Hand-wringing or playing with things in your pocket make you seem nervous.

- **Facial expressions.** How you really feel and the mood you're in is written all over your face. A smile says "welcome." A nod says, "yes, I understand." In the U.S., eye contact shows confidence and trustworthiness, while shifty eyes are considered nervous or sly. Frowning and staring can make people feel uneasy.

*G*rooming

You could be wearing the most professional-looking designer suit, but you can destroy your entire image if your hair is in disarray, your nails are chipped, you have a food stain on your blouse or tie, or your breath is bad.

Before you get dressed, check over your clothing. Is everything clean and well-pressed? Are there any food or perspiration stains? lint? dog or cat hairs? missing buttons? Are your shoes free of scuffs and soil?

After getting dressed and before going out the door, take a good, hard look at yourself in a full-length mirror in a well-lit room.
Women: Are there any runs in your stockings or lipstick on your teeth?
Men: Do you see any "five-o'clock shadow"?

Even if you have to get up a little earlier in the morning, make sure you have sufficient time to take care of any last-minute grooming emergencies. If you roll right out of bed, into your clothes, and out the door, you're going to look as if you have.

Check your appearance periodically throughout the day for the stray piece of lunchtime spinach that may remain between your teeth, the occasional coffee or ink stain, or blotchy makeup.

Professional Dress

What you choose to wear says a great deal about your personality, attitude, and professionalism. Select your business wardrobe with an eye toward enhancing your professional image.

Avoid clothing and accessories that are "too" anything. Clothes that are too short, too tight, or too gaudy may call attention to you, but not in a positive way. Avoid anything that's exaggerated or overdone, whether it's your clothing, jewelry, hairstyle, or makeup.

Watch what others around you are wearing. Paying particular attention to the clothing choices of people in your organization whom you consider to be successful will give you an idea of what's accepted—and expected—in your office. Then adapt those general guidelines to your own personal style. The idea is to fit in, not become a carbon copy.

Whatever your current position within your organization, dress for the position you'd like to attain. Your appearance has a major impact on the way you feel and perform. If you're confident, you feel competent. Appearance also has a big impact on how others, including co-workers, clients, customers, and supervisors, view you. It's never too soon in your career to begin to cultivate your professional image. Aim high.

When selecting a business wardrobe, remember that simple and basic are best. Choose colors that flatter and pieces that can be mixed and matched for maximum variety at minimum cost. Opt for fewer "good" (well-made, classically styled) pieces rather than a closet full of pieces of lesser quality.

Every piece in your business wardrobe should meet the following criteria:

1. **Appropriateness.** Is it right for the job, company, season, region, climate, and setting?

2. **Fit.** Is it the correct size? Does it flatter you without calling undue attention to your body?

3. **Message.** Does it show good judgment as well as good taste? Does it say "I'm a professional who should be taken seriously?"

Business Casual

It used to be that the only time casual dress was acceptable in business situations was at company-sponsored picnics, golf tournaments, or other recreational or social events. Today, however, many companies allow and even encourage a more relaxed dress code with formally sanctioned "Dress Down Days" on either an occasional or a regular basis.

The thought of being able to dress casually and comfortably for work may be appealing, but don't get too carried away. Keep in mind that "dress down" doesn't mean sloppy. There's never a right time to wear your ripped jeans, short shorts, tank tops, muscle shirts, or T-shirts emblazoned with your favorite political slogans.

Business casual is exactly that—business. Therefore, you need to put as much (and sometimes even more) thought into your casual wardrobe as you do into your regular business wardrobe. And there's never any excuse for careless grooming!

First, consider some generalities about selecting your business casual wardrobe. Like any business attire, it should be well-fitting, flattering, clean, and pressed. The accompanying chart provides some specific guidelines.

Guidelines for Business Casual Dress

Women

Acceptable attire can include skirts, split skirts (skorts), or well-fitting slacks with blouses or blouse/jacket combinations. Flat shoes with stockings are okay, but not sneakers or sandals unless you'll be attending a sporting event.

Men

Acceptable attire can include slacks with shirts, collared cotton T-shirts, or sweaters. Loafers and slip-on shoes with socks (no sneakers or sandals unless you're attending a sporting event) are appropriate.

Both

If jeans are appropriate for the setting and occasion, make sure they're free of holes or tatters. Again, no cut-offs.

3

Networking

Never underestimate or forget the importance of establishing and maintaining an extensive network of contacts. In business, there's a certain amount of truth to the old adage, "Your success often depends as much on who you know as what you know." The contacts you make today can open doors for you throughout your career.

Many people are intimidated at the prospect of networking. If you're one of these people, think of it this way: You've been doing it all your life without even realizing it. Everyone you've ever met and everyone you know is part of a network that you've built up—friends, current and former co-workers, neighbors, social or sports club members, your doctor, dentist, banker, accountant, religious leader, customers, competitors. That's a lot of people! And they're all part of your personal network.

Now that you know you have so many networking opportunities, learn to direct your efforts to achieve your professional goals. Keep your eyes open at all times for networking occasions. They're just about everywhere—even where you'd least expect to find them.

Here are some opportunities for networking within your organization:

- **Join company sports teams.** Don't worry if you're not a pro. Learn as much as possible about the activity, come equipped, and have fun!

- **Look outside your own position or department.** Volunteer to assist with company-wide events or activities. This is a great way to demonstrate your versatility as well as your "team spirit."

- **Don't eat lunch alone at your desk.** If you do, you're missing the opportunity to get to know your colleagues on a more relaxed, informal basis. Besides, everybody needs a break now and then!

There's a big world out there. Get out and circulate! Here are
some ways you can create networking opportunities outside the
office:

- **Join organizations and be an active participant.** Your
  professional or trade organizations are obvious choices. But
  don't overlook other opportunities such as your local
  chamber of commerce or interest or social groups that
  focus on a particular area such as gourmet dining or
  English literature. Speak up at meetings, participate on
  committees, attend the events.

- **Volunteer.** Become involved with a charitable organization
  or cause in your community. Don't just write a check; give
  of your time. An extra bonus is the good feeling you'll get
  from helping others.

Although networking can be a powerful tool for making new
contacts and a source of new personal and professional
relationships, certain protocols do govern networking situations.

The Do's and Don'ts of Working a Room

"Working a room" doesn't mean flitting from person to person,
pumping hands, and giving out your business card. It doesn't
mean scanning the room for bigger and better opportunities when
you're already in the midst of a conversation.

It simply means being alert for networking opportunities. It means
keeping your eyes—and your mind—open.

If you're attending a party or event where you know the host or someone else, take advantage of any offers they may extend to introduce you. If you don't receive any such offers or if there's a particular person or group of people you'd like to meet, it's perfectly appropriate to ask for an introduction.

But what if you walk into a party or event and find that you don't know another soul in the room? First of all, don't panic. Then consider your options.

Option number one is to find the farthest out-of-the-way corner and hide there for the duration of the event. Option number two is to stand there and hope someone comes up to you. Option number three is to find someone else who is alone, approach that person with a friendly smile, and introduce yourself.

If you choose option number one, you practically guarantee yourself a miserable time. If you choose option number two, you could find yourself standing alone and feeling very awkward for quite a while. If you choose option number three, congratulations! You've recognized and taken advantage of a prime networking opportunity.

If the idea of approaching a total stranger makes you uncomfortable, remember that you're probably doing that person a favor by initiating conversation. There aren't many people who actually enjoy standing alone in a crowded room.

Initiating a conversation can be a relatively simple and painless process if you prepare ahead. Have your most professional handshake and ten-second self-introduction ready. Look the person in the eye. Ask a question or use one of the other "opening lines" suggested in Chapter 1.

If the two of you "click," be sure to exchange business cards before you part company. Before you file the card when you get back to your home or office, note on it where you met the person and any other pertinent information.

Of course, networking isn't always foolproof. Sometimes, despite your best efforts, you will run into people you genuinely don't like or don't want to see again. In those cases, the best thing to do is cut the conversation short in a polite, yet firm way. "It was nice meeting you, but I must be going now" is a good way to bow out. And, no matter how you feel about the person, don't forget to smile and say good-bye.

Networking Etiquette

So far, this chapter has focused on how networking can help you. But, to be truly effective, it can't be totally one-sided. Networking works best when it works both ways. Just as you depend on the people in your network for support and assistance, they should be able to expect the same from you. Reciprocating is one of the "golden" rules of networking etiquette.

You can initiate networking contacts in a number of ways. As described earlier in this chapter, you can expand your network simply by taking advantage of opportunities to introduce yourself to new people at parties or events.

Depending on the circumstances, your relationship with the individual (or someone who knows the individual and is willing to provide an introduction), and what feels comfortable to you, you can also initiate contact by writing a letter or placing a phone call.

If you're following up on a referral, be sure to mention the name of your mutual acquaintance at the beginning of your note or call.

But before you initiate contact, determine your personal objectives. Are you looking for a promotion? A new job? Think about what you want this new contact to know about you. If necessary, make a list of the points you want to cover.

At the same time, show a genuine interest in what the other person has to say. Even if this person can't help you get a particular job or promotion, he or she could be a mentor, providing invaluable advice and guidance throughout your career.

Don't just focus on your own needs and goals. Listen for clues that can help you discover how you might assist the other person. Once you've offered a helping hand, it's much easier to ask for one in return sometime down the line.

Follow up the initial contact with a brief note. If the person has provided information or other assistance, be sure to express your thanks. Otherwise, just let the person know you appreciate the time spent talking to you.

Once you've established the connection, keep it alive. If you see a magazine or newspaper article that might interest the person, send it along with a brief personal note. Acknowledge awards, promotions, or positive publicity your contact has received. Call just to say "hello" and, if possible, get together for lunch.

Remember, business cards sitting in a Rolodex or database don't constitute a network. They're just pieces of paper unless you put in the time and effort to keep the personal connection going.

4

The Job Interview

If there's any situation that can test your ability to function gracefully and professionally under pressure, it's the job interview. While some interviewers go out of their way to make candidates feel as comfortable as possible, others like to apply extra pressure to help them determine who has what it takes. Book and movie character Forrest Gump, compared life to a box of chocolates, observing "You never know what you're going to get." The same can be said for job interviews.

While every job interview may be different, you can't go wrong if you follow the general guidelines discussed in this chapter.

*B*efore the Interview

Although you make your impression *during* the interview, what you do beforehand often determines whether or not that impression is a favorable one. Here are some areas you shouldn't overlook as you prepare for that all-important meeting:

- **Do your homework.** Find out everything you can about the company. Ask for brochures and an annual report, if one's available. Look in the library for articles about the company.

- **Think about your appearance.** Select clothing that reflects your professionalism. Pay close attention to your grooming. (For more details on wardrobe and grooming, see Chapter 2.)

- **Practice.** Some interviewers begin by inviting the candidate to "tell me about yourself." Be ready to offer a brief verbal resumé, paying special attention to the work experience and job skills that pertain to the position you're being interviewed for. If possible, ask a friend to role-play with you.

- **Prepare your resumé and references.** Be ready to answer questions about your resumé. For example, "How long did you work at XYZ Corporation?" or "Why did you leave your last job?" Have names and telephone numbers of references ready to offer. Be sure you've asked permission to use people as references before you include them.

During the Interview

From the moment you walk in the door, make sure your image says "professional." Here are some actions that are not only appropriate during an interview, but also necessary for creating a positive impression.

- **Be on time.** If possible, leave yourself an extra ten minutes in case you have problems with parking, finding the elevator, or locating the right office. Use any leftover time to check your appearance one last time.

- **Shake hands.** If the interviewer doesn't offer his or her hand, you should. (For more on the art of handshaking, see Chapter 1.) Make sure your handshake is firm and confident. And don't forget to smile and make eye contact.

- **Wait to be seated.** If the interviewer doesn't offer you a seat, ask where you should sit.

- **Show your confidence.** Sit up straight and tall in your chair. Look the interviewer in the eye. Don't fidget or squirm. Speak clearly. Keep your hands away from your mouth.

- **Emphasize your strengths.** Tell the interviewer exactly why you are the best candidate for the position.

- **Keep your answers brief and to the point.** Don't ramble or stray off on unrelated tangents. Answer the interviewer's questions in a straightforward, honest manner.

- **Keep your cool.** No matter what the interviewer asks you, don't act annoyed or become antagonized. If the question is inappropriate and you truly don't wish to answer it, you can always calmly and politely ask the interviewer how the answer to that question pertains to the position. If you're still uncomfortable, you can hold your ground by stating that you would be happy to discuss any information that would help determine your qualifications and interest in the position.

- **Ask for the job.** This isn't the time to act coy. It's not attractive or effective. Let the interviewer know you're interested in the position and state your reasons why.

- **Establish the "next step."** Ask the interviewer when he or she expects a decision to be made and when you might expect to be contacted. If the interviewer needs more information from you, set a definite time when you will provide it.

- **End on a positive note.** Even if you decide you don't want the position after all, smile, shake hands, and thank the interviewer pleasantly.

After the Interview

Once you leave the interview, proper etiquette demands that you send a note of thanks for being extended the interview opportunity. It's also perfectly acceptable to follow up with a phone call, within certain guidelines.

- **Send a thank you note immediately.** Reiterate your interest in the position and reemphasize some of the main reasons why you're the best candidate for the job. If you're not interested in the job, send a note thanking the interviewer for his or her time. It's the polite thing to do—and you never know when another, more appealing, position may open up at the same company.

- **Call to follow up.** If the interviewer has told you that a decision about the position should be made within a week, check in at the end of the week. If you learn that you didn't get the position, try to get some feedback from the interviewer. It may not be what you want to hear, but it could be of great value to you in preparing for future interviews. Don't make a nuisance of yourself by phoning every day, however.

5

Business Dining

Sure, you know better than to put your elbows on the table or to reach across someone else's plate to grab the salt shaker, but are your "company manners" polished enough to stand up to the challenge of the business lunch or dinner? Dining together gives people a chance to get to know one another outside the confines of the office. But don't let the setting fool you. Whether you're the host or the guest, business is still the first item on the menu.

33

*B*usiness Dining Options: Breakfast, Lunch, or Dinner?

These days people who want to conduct business over a meal choose lunch more frequently than they do breakfast or dinner. That's because lunch is usually the most practical and comfortable option for most people. Since it occurs during the business day, a lunchtime meeting eliminates the awkwardness of considering outside-of-work obligations.

Dinners, even if business is going to be discussed, are generally expected to be more social in nature. The invitation may include spouses or significant others. If so, it's only polite to keep the conversation general and away from "hard core" business. Otherwise, you risk making nonparticipants feel left out and awkward.

If a brief meeting is on the agenda, a business breakfast can nicely fill the bill. Business breakfasts are becoming increasingly popular because they generally take less time than other meals. Some organizations even schedule breakfasts before official business hours begin so no time is lost from the workday.

Hosting a Business Lunch

As noted, when it comes to doing business, lunch is often the meal of choice. But don't, for even one moment, make the mistake of confusing the business lunch with your run-of-the-mill mid-day repast. No cafeteria vending machine or restaurant fast-food fare will do here. Real mind-your-manners restaurant dining is in order. And, by the way, if you do the inviting, that makes you the host. That means you make the plans—and you pay the bill.

Hosting a business lunch takes a certain amount of thought and planning. Like any other business or social event, there are a number of essential factors to consider such as location, food, and comfort.

Before planning a business lunch, think about your reason for wanting to host it. Is your objective to court a prospective client or to enhance your relationship with a current client? Will you be interviewing an employment prospect, or rewarding your staff for a job well done? Are you celebrating a holiday, or an individual milestone such as a retirement or employment anniversary? A business lunch can even substitute for an in-office meeting or provide a pleasant way to cultivate your network.

Many companies and organizations have specific guidelines—sometimes written, sometimes simply passed along via word-of-mouth—regarding appropriate reasons and occasions, frequency, and protocol of business lunches. For example, one insurance company had a policy to entertain clients only *after* they had purchased policies. When a representative who was unfamiliar with the policy took some prospective clients to lunch *before* they had formalized their purchase, he was reprimanded. Be sure you know your company's guidelines. If you're not sure, ask.

Choosing the Restaurant

Once you've established the appropriateness of the lunch, it's time to choose the setting. It's a good idea to set up a file of restaurants that are business-friendly in terms of atmosphere, clientele, and service. Try out new restaurants or restaurants you haven't visited for six or more months before you bring business guests.

Sometimes you may find yourself hosting a lunch in a town other than your own. If possible, do some research before you get there. If not, ask the concierge at your hotel to suggest some suitable restaurants. And, of course, it's appropriate—and even extra considerate—to ask your guest if he or she has any favorite spots.

When selecting a restaurant, consider your guest. The location should be convenient for him or her. Keep in mind any specific dietary requirements or food preferences. If you're not sure of either, pick a restaurant that offers a wide range of selections.

Inviting Your Guests

Call your guest at least one week and, if possible, two weeks in advance to schedule a mutually agreeable date and time for lunch. Just because you're free next Friday at noon, don't assume your guest will be too. Be prepared to offer a few alternative dates and times.

Ask whether your guest has any particular preferences regarding food or even the restaurant itself. Be open and flexible.

Let your guest know if you're planning to invite any other people to join you at lunch. It's also a good idea to mention whether there's a specific topic you'd like to discuss so your guest can prepare appropriate information and bring along any necessary materials.

Making the Reservations

A couple of minutes spent telephoning in a reservation to the restaurant can save untold time—and embarrassment—on the day of your business lunch. No matter how charming a host you are or how congenial the guest, no one wants to waste precious time waiting in a busy restaurant for a table to become available.

In addition to the time and date of your lunch, tell the restaurant how many people you expect to be in your party. You may also wish to specify whether you want your table to be located in a smoking or non-smoking section. If anyone in your party has a physical disability requiring special accommodations, mention that as well.

Greeting Your Guests

Make sure your guest knows how to get to the restaurant. Most people appreciate it when you offer parking information as well.

If you haven't met your guest face to face before, offer a description of yourself. To make it as easy as possible for your guest to identify you, tell your guest the color of the coat or clothing you expect to wear as well as your height and hair color.

Arrive early. Immediately check in at the reservation desk to confirm your reservation. Then, wait in the lobby for your guest to arrive.

If there are a number of people in your party, try to wait until everyone has arrived before you ask to be seated. However, it isn't polite to keep everyone waiting for one or two guests who haven't arrived ten minutes or more after the appointed meeting time. In this case, it's proper to escort the other members of your party to the table, arrange for them to be seated, and order drinks. Be sure to inform the reservation desk of your location so your late-arriving guests can join you.

Ordering

"Good afternoon, my name is Chris. I'll be your server today." In reality, Chris is much more. Your server is someone who can be very helpful in making your business lunch a success.

Take a good look at your server so you can easily and quickly recognize him or her later if you have a problem or request.

If your server doesn't offer his or her name, don't snap your fingers, stand up and wave frantically, or shout out "Honey," "Sweetie," or "Garcon" to attract his or her attention. With a little patience, you can usually request service by catching your server's eye or with a discrete wave of the fingers. If all else fails, say "waiter" or "waitress" in a calm and gentle voice.

Ordering cocktails or wine. Before taking your lunch order, your server will probably ask if you and your guest would like a drink. The best way to handle this is to defer to your guest. If your guest orders a drink, you may too. If your guest doesn't want one, don't. And always keep in mind that the three-martini lunch has disappeared. Drinking is not a mandatory part of the business meal and, in fact, may have a negative impact on your ability to think and function in your most professional manner.

Should your guest indicate a preference for wine, don't be intimidated. A good basic guideline to remember is that white wine generally goes with fish or fowl and red goes with meat. Remember, this is only a guideline, not a hard-and-fast rule. Like everything else, wine is a matter of personal taste.

It's never polite to push wine or any alcoholic beverage on a guest who doesn't want it. It's also perfectly appropriate for you to order a non-alcoholic beverage for yourself if you prefer not to drink. Just remember that if wine is being served as part of the meal and you would rather not have any, don't turn your wine glass upside down. Simply say, "No, thank you."

Ordering food. You may know the restaurant's menu by heart. But give your guest sufficient "quiet time" to review it. You might briefly make some suggestions about some of the restaurant's specialties.

Allow your guest to order first and follow his or her lead. For instance, if your guest orders soup or a salad, so should you.

When it comes to ordering, the less fuss the better. In other words, don't grill your server about what's in each dish or how it's prepared. Of course, if you have certain allergies or other dietary restrictions, you may make inquiries and requests to accommodate them. But do so as simply and as reasonably as possible.

Avoid ordering foods that you know will be messy or difficult to eat. Even if the restaurant serves the best spaghetti or French onion soup, wait for a non-business visit to order it.

Paying the Check

It's been said before, but it's worth repeating: if you're the host, you're responsible for paying the check. This is proper etiquette whether you are a man or a woman.

What isn't proper etiquette is playing tug-of-war with the bill. If a male guest is uncomfortable with his female host paying the bill, a polite, non-argumentative approach would be for her to say, "The XYZ Corporation would like you to be our guest."

To avoid the problem altogether, the host may make payment arrangements in advance of the lunch. That way, the bill will not be presented in front of the guest.

You may quietly review the bill, but don't pull out your calculator to check the addition. If you find any errors, don't cause a commotion at the table. Calmly excuse yourself and take the bill to the server's station to resolve the problem.

If possible, pay by credit card. It's the quickest and most discrete means of settling the bill. If you do pay cash, you may ask for a receipt for business purposes.

Don't make a production out of calculating the tip. But do check the bill to see if it's already included (especially if you are dining with a large party).

A typical tip is 15 to 20 percent of the total bill. This can be easily calculated by figuring 10 percent, and then adding half or double that amount. If a person other than your server took the order (that person is called a captain), add another 5 percent for that person.

Guidelines for tipping other restaurant service personnel are as follows:

Sommelier (wine steward)	$3 to $5 per bottle or 15 percent of the cost of the wine
Coatroom Attendant	$1 per coat
Garage Attendant	$1 to $2

The tip for the server and sommelier may be included in your credit card total. Or you may leave the server's tip in cash on the table. Other service personnel such as coatroom and garage attendants should be paid directly. It is also polite to say "thank you" for services rendered.

Table Manners

Whether you're the host or the guest, good table manners are a *must* at any business dining occasion. Table manners weren't invented to make dining more difficult. Quite the contrary. They should make it more pleasant by ensuring that no one's behavior offends anyone.

Most of what you have to know about proper behavior at the table is really just common sense—and common decency. Keep these guidelines in mind:

- **Be polite.** Wait until after the meal is ordered before discussing business. When food is passed to you, say "please" and "thank you." Don't put your handbag or briefcase on the table. Put it in your lap or on the floor. Wait until everyone has been served before eating (unless the host insists that you begin before the food gets cold).

- **Be neat.** Chew with your mouth closed. Wait until you've swallowed before speaking. Don't gesture with a utensil in your hand—especially if it has food on it. When eating bread or rolls, break off one piece at a time and butter it as you're ready to eat it. Don't butter the entire piece of bread or roll at one time. Try to avoid ordering messy foods. If you drop a utensil, ask the server for a replacement.

- **Be pleasant.** Don't complain about the food or criticize the service.

- **Be considerate.** Although it's important to check your grooming throughout the day, the dining table is not the proper place to do it. If you want to comb your hair or reapply your lipstick before leaving the restaurant, by all means do so, but in the restroom, not at the table.

If you're a smoker, don't assume that your guest will want to sit in the "smoking" section. Some people have allergies or simply find cigarette smoke offensive while they're eating. As a polite host, you should refrain from smoking unless your guest smokes. As a polite guest, you should ask your host's permission before lighting up. It's never appropriate to smoke during a meal. Wait until everyone has finished or almost finished eating.

Correct Use of Dishes and Utensils

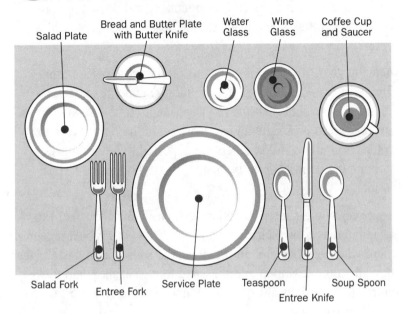

Salad Plate | Bread and Butter Plate with Butter Knife | Water Glass | Wine Glass | Coffee Cup and Saucer

Salad Fork | Entree Fork | Service Plate | Teaspoon | Entree Knife | Soup Spoon

Given the popularity of fast food and other ultra-casual dining establishments, it's no surprise that so many people panic at the sight of place settings consisting of multiple plates, knives, forks, and spoons. But there's really no need for alarm. Just keep the following basic guidelines in mind:

- **Food dishes (including bread and butter plate) are on the left.** An easy way to remember is to keep in mind that both "food" and "left" have four letters.

- **Beverage containers (including coffee cup and saucer) are on the right.** Both "drink" and "right" have five letters.

Ah, but what about those utensils? That daunting array of salad, entree, and dessert forks and soup, coffee, and dessert spoons. How can you tell which is which and, just as important, which is yours?

Actually, there are several variations on the basic place setting. The most correct, although not the most commonly used in the United States, is the *Outside-In* place setting. In this setting, forks are on the left and knife and spoons are on the right. The name comes from the fact that diners are expected to work their way through the utensils, from both sides, from the outside to the inside.

To be ready to face any variation with grace and style, learn to identify utensils by their shape and size. That way, you'll recognize them wherever they are! For instance, the soup spoon has a bigger bowl than the teaspoon and the salad fork is smaller than the entree fork. And, as always, if in doubt, observe your host or others around you.

Oops! Despite all your prior preparation and careful observation, you've used your entree fork to eat your salad. Don't make an issue of it. Many times, you can substitute another utensil in your place setting for the one you've used. Or, without drawing undue attention to yourself, quietly ask for a replacement.

Now that you're familiar with the do's and don'ts of business dining, read on for some tips on a related topic: business entertaining.

6

*E*ntertaining

You know you have to be on your best professional behavior when meeting with a client, prospect, or supervisor in the office conference room or in an elegant restaurant. But what about when the setting is a concert, the company picnic or office party, a sporting event, or some other "unofficial" locale?

No matter how casual the setting or how festive the occasion, it's still business. Yes, a day at the ballpark is a great way for you and your client, supervisor, or colleague to get to know one another better outside the formal confines of the office. But keep in mind that your behavior at today's ballgame is the behavior your companion will remember at tomorrow's board meeting.

Be yourself at your very best. Dress appropriately. Be a congenial companion. Maintain a positive attitude. And, above all, smile and enjoy yourself. Believe it or not, you can make a good impression and still have a good time.

When You're the Host

Whatever the event or circumstances, your first duty as a host is to make sure your guest has a good time. This may require a little pre-event planning on your part in terms of providing transportation and arranging for tickets or other types of seating.

If you're taking your guest to the opera or a hockey game and have never attended one before, learn everything you can about opera or hockey before you go. That way, you can hold an intelligent conversation with your guest. Understanding what you are seeing will also enhance your enjoyment.

If, instead of being a spectator, you will be expected to be a participant—in a game of golf, for instance—be sure you know the rules, have the correct equipment, and brush up on your skills.

Once you arrive at the event, make sure your guest is comfortable. If appropriate, provide food and drinks. If the event is a party, make sure all necessary introductions are made.

Whatever the event, make sure your reactions to whatever is happening on the field or on stage are appropriate. Even if your favorite team is losing in the play-off game, refrain from booing, hissing, or "coaching" from the stands. At a play or concert, applaud only when appropriate.

Be a good listener. Invite your guest to talk about himself or herself. This can give you some valuable insight as to his or her interests, family, and personality.

The Office Party

There are two ways you don't want to be remembered after an office party. First, you don't want to be remembered for becoming the center of attention by dancing with a lampshade on your head. You can avoid being remembered for your "colorful" behavior by following this simple advice: *Don't get drunk.* Even if you think you can "hold your liquor," limit your consumption. You may not have complete control over everything you say or do while under the influence. But you will be held accountable.

Second, you don't want to be remembered as the person who snubbed your colleagues by not showing up. So, make sure you show up. Attendance at the company office party isn't optional. Whether you believe it or not, your absence will be noticed—and noted.

Get there on time. Making a late entrance won't make everyone think you're important. It will only make people think you're rude.

Be cordial. Smile and be friendly to everyone. Take advantage of the opportunity to expand your network. Initiate conversations with people outside your existing circle of immediate co-workers and friends. Keep business talk to a minimum.

Don't initiate or participate in office gossip. And don't make yourself the subject of tomorrow's office gossip by flirting.

Off-color or offensive jokes and stories aren't appropriate under any circumstances. Don't tell them yourself or encourage others to tell them.

Say hello to the boss. Use your most engaging small-talk techniques. Be pleasant, but respectful.

If you don't usually call your boss by his or her first name, don't start now.

Even if the party is dull and you're dying to make your escape ten minutes after you arrive, stay around for an appropriate length of time. And be conscious of your body language. It's very bad manners to let people see how bored you are.

After the party, send a thank you note to the organizers.

Socializing With Colleagues

Actually, you can apply the guidelines described in the "Office Party" section to any social encounter with your colleagues. As with the office party, your attendance is expected. Of course, that doesn't mean you have to leave your spouse and children alone every Friday night to go drinking with your colleagues. It only means you should make a point to join in the outside-of-work activities every once in a while, even if it's only to accompany your co-workers when they go out to lunch.

Be discrete about making any major personal revelations. An evening out with the office gang is not the time to play true confessions. At the same time, refrain from judging or criticizing anyone else. For instance, if your co-worker has a fight with his or her spouse, don't offer your opinion or advice.

Which brings the subject once again to alcohol. Drinking too much can make you drop your guard and loosen your tongue. Don't feel that you have to keep downing drinks to show that you're one of the gang. You can be sociable and still remain sober. Once you've reached your limit, switch to something non-alcoholic.

If family or significant others are included in the outing, brief them in advance about what is appropriate in terms of dress, conversation, and, if necessary, general behavior. Remember, their actions and words reflect on you.

7

"Living Together" in the Workplace

Just as you are a citizen of the country you live in, you are also a citizen of the office you work in. And as a citizen, you have certain rights along with certain responsibilities to your fellow citizens.

Coexisting with others in peace and harmony isn't always easy. Especially when you're sharing a copier, coffee machine, and conference room. But it can be done. All it takes is a little common courtesy when it comes to using shared territory and equipment, and a little respect for other people's personal space and sensibilities.

Equipment Etiquette

There are seven basic equipment etiquette rules to remember:

- **Rule #1: If it's empty, fill it.**

  The coffee pot's empty again. The copier's out of toner. The fax is out of paper. It makes you angry, doesn't it?

  Remember that anger the next time you drink the last of the coffee or notice the toner level is low or the fax paper tray is empty. Use it positively to make yourself a better citizen of your office. You don't have to be Julia Child to make a pot of coffee. And you don't have to be an electronics genius to know when the fax needs paper.

  It takes only a few minutes to fill a paper tray or make a pot of coffee. Don't use "But I don't know how" as an excuse. Ask someone to help you.

- **Rule #2: If it's broken, fix it. Or at least get it fixed.**

  From time to time, machines break down. If you're the one using the machine at the time, don't just walk away and hope the next person will think he or she did it.

  Even if you didn't break it in the first place, take care of it anyway. Quibbling about blame and responsibility is counterproductive, not to mention totally unprofessional.

- **Rule #3: If you don't know how to use it properly, learn.**

  Misuse of equipment is more than just a time-waster. It can also damage sensitive machinery. So before you push that button or turn that dial, make sure you know what you're doing.

- **Rule #4: If it isn't your turn, wait.**

  Sure, you're in a hurry. And you've got to use the copier right now to make five hundred copies for your meeting in ten minutes. Well, get in line, because the person ahead of you at the copy machine has a meeting in five minutes.

  Next time, give yourself a little more time. If you work in a busy office, you're bound to run into a traffic jam at some crucial machine at one time or another.

  Of course, if you're running a large job and someone needs to make a few copies, it's common courtesy to let that person use the machine. Next time the person with the few copies to make may be you.

- **Rule #5: If it isn't yours, don't read it.**

  If you find someone else's original in the copy machine or a transmission addressed to your co-worker in the fax machine, resist the temptation to gather some inside information or juicy gossip by reading the document. Once you have determined who the original belongs to or the fax message is addressed to, put it in that person's mailbox.

The "don't read it" rule also applies to data displayed on someone else's computer screen, and mail lying on someone else's desk.

- **Rule #6: If you make a mess, clean it up.**

  Pick up your own trash; wipe up your own spills. Take all your originals and other papers with you when you leave the area.

- **Rule #7: If you're finished with it, make sure it's ready for the next person to use.**

  Reset the copier to the standard one copy, 8 1/2" x 11" size. Don't change computer programming or automatic dial numbers on the fax machine without permission.

In addition to these seven basic rules that apply to all equipment, each piece of machinery also has its own specific etiquette considerations.

Fax Machines

Equipment etiquette doesn't only apply to your own office. Your courtesy should also extend to the people on the receiving end of your transmissions. Don't send unsolicited faxes. Many people view them as even worse than junk mail because they waste paper and tie up valuable machine time.

Whenever possible, avoid faxing during peak hours. Choose times when usage is traditionally lighter: early morning, at lunch time, or after official working hours. A bonus is that off-peak transmissions can save your company money if you're faxing long-distance.

Never send restricted-access materials without obtaining prior permission. You can't guarantee that the person who retrieves the message is always the person it is addressed to.

Make sure your cover sheet is complete and coherent. The fax cover sheet should include the name, department, fax number, and phone number of both the recipient and the sender; the time and date sent; the number of pages; any message; and whether or not the delivery is urgent.

If the recipient uses a shared fax, call and give notice when you've sent a transmission.

Copiers

Even if company policy allows you to use the copier for personal use, don't do it during peak usage hours. If you're running a large personal job, don't use up the company's paper. Bring your own.

Sharing Space With Others

Unless you work in a one-person office, you'll need to observe certain protocols when it comes to sharing space with co-workers. Many of the "rules" in this area are simple courtesies.

Someone Else's Space

No matter how closely people live or work together, all employees need a place to call their own. While offices, desks, and file cabinets are officially company property, they are temporarily "owned" by the people who use them and should be treated accordingly.

Just as you wouldn't walk into anyone's home unannounced, you shouldn't walk into anyone's office without knocking. Even if the door is open, wait until the person asks you to come in. If the person is on the telephone, wait until he or she is finished.

You should also ask permission before borrowing, moving, or using equipment in a person's office. If the other person isn't present when you use the equipment, make sure you put everything back the way you found it when you're finished.

Shared Space

The cafeteria, copy room, restrooms, and conference room don't really "belong" to any one person. So, who's responsible for keeping them in good condition?

Actually, you are—along with everybody else who uses them. It really doesn't have to be a big deal. In most cases, it's just a matter of cleaning up after yourself.

Sometimes a little bit of pre-planning is required. For instance, if you want to use the conference room, you may have to schedule it in advance. This is for your benefit as much as anyone's. After all, how would you like to be ready to begin your meeting and find that the conference room is already in use?

Find out the proper scheduling procedures and follow them. Be as flexible as possible. If a conflict occurs, try to resolve the problem calmly, politely, and discretely.

Smoking in shared spaces can also present some etiquette problems—both for the smokers and the non-smokers in the building. Many offices now provide non-smoking areas or are completely smoke-free. Ignoring your company's smoking policy is more than bad manners. It indicates a lack of respect for authority and a disregard for your co-workers' health.

If you're not sure about company policy, ask. In any case, ask permission from the individuals you are with at the time.

Your Space

Even though you're the one who "lives" there, your office, cubicle, or desk area is more than an expression of your personality. It's a reflection on your company.

You really never know who's going to be passing by or stopping in, so make sure your space is always neat and organized. Personal items can make your office feel more comfortable and homey, but make sure they fit your company's guidelines for decoration and are in good taste.

Door Etiquette

Once upon a time, it was considered proper etiquette for a man to open the door for a woman. It still is. However, today, it's just as proper for a woman to open a door for a man.

Gender should not be the deciding factor in determining who opens the door, goes through it first, or holds it open for someone else. Nor should corporate status or age. The determining factor should be good old common courtesy.

Under ordinary circumstances, if you're the first person to get to the door, you should be the one to open it and go through it first. Be sure to hold the door until the next person is able to grab it. Allowing a door to slam in someone's face is impolite and dangerous.

If someone needs help, offer it.

Although these are the guidelines that apply in today's work world, for some people, old habits—and old etiquette practices— die hard. So, if a man insists on holding the door for a woman, chances are he simply hasn't read this book and truly believes he is demonstrating correct behavior. The polite and professional woman will not view this act as a challenge to her independence and physical capabilities. She won't launch into a tirade on the equality of women in the workplace. Embarrassing another person is never good manners. Appreciate the gracious intent of the gesture. Smile. And don't forget to say "thank you."

8

The Telephone

These days, opportunity usually doesn't knock. More often than not, it calls first. So it's crucial that you—and your company—handle every call with the utmost competence, professionalism, and courtesy.

Receiving a Call

Good telephone etiquette begins before you even say "hello." Calls should be answered within three rings.

No matter what you're doing or how hassled you are, once you pick up the phone, your voice and manners should bespeak professionalism and your readiness to be of service to the caller. Take a deep breath before you pick up the phone. And smile. It may feel silly at first, but the smile on your face usually comes through in your voice as well.

Clearly identify yourself using your full name. Include a verb to avoid sounding abrupt. For example, "Jane Smith speaking" or "This is Jane Smith" instead of just "Jane Smith."

If you share a phone, be sure to include the department name. For example, "Marketing, Jane Smith speaking."

If the call is coming from the outside, include your company name. For example, "XYZ Manufacturing, Jane Smith speaking. How may I help you?"

Screening Calls

Sometimes you may be too busy to take phone calls. There's nothing wrong with asking your secretary to screen your calls as long as you're not in for some people and out for others.

If you don't wish to be disturbed, the secretary should say: "Mr. Evans isn't available right now. Is there anything I can help you with?" However, whether you're available or not, callers should never be put through the third degree before they're allowed to talk to you.

Call-back Courtesy

When it comes to returning telephone calls, the rule is easy to remember: the sooner the better and always within twenty-four hours. If you can't return the call yourself within a reasonable period of time, have someone else return it for you. Even if you can't help the caller, it's polite to call back and let that person know so he or she will have an opportunity to look elsewhere for the needed information.

If you use voice mail to answer your calls, include in your message the time you expect to return. If co-workers answer your phone, be sure they have accurate information about your anticipated return time.

When you tell someone you will call at a particular time, you have scheduled an appointment. The same is true when you arrange for someone to call you at a particular time. Just as you would not simply ignore an appointment to meet someone somewhere, you should never "stand up" a telephone appointment.

If you know you're going to be unavailable at the prescheduled time, call to let the person know. Or, at least have someone else call for you. Reschedule the call. Make sure you apologize for any inconvenience and thank the person for his or her understanding.

*D*uring the Conversation

No matter what else is going on around you, when you're on the telephone, your focus should be on the caller. That means no side conversations with co-workers. If you're talking to someone in your office and the phone begins to ring, finish your conversation before picking up the receiver.

To avoid distractions, do everything possible to keep background noises to a minimum. Turn off the radio. Shut the window. If people around you are talking, move to another area, if possible.

Concentrate on listening. That means no doodling, typing, straightening papers, cleaning out your desk, typing on a keyboard, or planning your lunch order. Be responsive to the caller's statements and questions. A well-placed "I see" or "Uh-huh" now and then lets the speaker know you're still awake and interested.

Put callers on hold only when it's absolutely necessary. Ask for permission first and wait for a response.

If you must put a caller on hold, make sure he or she doesn't languish there for long periods of time. When answering another call, put the first caller on hold only long enough to take a message. The first caller should always take priority.

Check back with the person on hold every twenty or thirty seconds. People tend to feel abandoned when left in "on-hold" limbo for too long. It's only common courtesy to provide periodic status reports. However, there is no excuse for leaving anyone on hold for long periods of time. If you can't help a person within a reasonable time, offer to call back.

Before transferring a call, give the caller the new extension number in case you get disconnected during the transfer. Don't put the call through without briefing the person to whom the call is being transferred. This gives the recipient of the call an opportunity to prepare for the needs and temperament of the caller. It also saves the caller the time and frustration of having to repeat his or her question or explanation.

When You're the Caller

Don't you just hate it when a caller who has dialed a wrong number slams the phone down in your ear without even a simple, "I'm sorry"? Remember that the next time you're the caller who dials the wrong number.

Besides being rude, hanging up without an apology can be bad for business. Don't assume that just because the person on the other end of the line can't see you, he or she can't find out who you are. Technology has made it possible to trace many calls by simply pressing a few buttons on the keypad. Some people even have devices that automatically display the phone numbers of all incoming calls.

Before you place any call, get yourself organized. Know what you want to accomplish and what you want to say. If you will be referring to certain materials, have them ready. If the other person will also need these materials, send or fax them ahead of time.

Immediately identify yourself to whoever answers the phone. If a secretary answers, you should include your complete name and company name. Just in case the secretary doesn't relay the information completely or correctly, repeat it when the client or customer answers.

Never assume that people will recognize your voice, no matter how many times you call or how well you think you know them.

You've already read that it's impolite to walk into someone's office without being invited. The same is true for "dropping in" via telephone. Briefly explain the purpose of your call and ask if the person has time to talk to you now. If the person is busy at the moment, ask when would be a better time to call back.

Speakerphones can be a great way to bring a group of people together for a conversation. However, be sure to let the person on the other end of the line know when you're using the speakerphone and immediately announce who is present in the room.

Know when—and how—to say "goodbye." When you have concluded with your business, close with a brief summary of how you plan to follow up. For instance, you could say, "I'll have that proposal to you on Monday." End with a positive statement such as, "It's been nice talking to you." Then say goodbye and gently hang up the phone—no slamming, please. And, oh yes, don't make any comments to anyone else in your work area until you've hung up. The other person may still be on the line.

Car Phones

Car phones weren't made for chatting with friends as you're driving down the highway at fifty-five miles an hour. You can't focus your full attention on driving when you're talking on the phone. And there's no way you can focus on a conversation while you're trying to safely negotiate your way through rush-hour traffic!

Whenever possible, wait until you're stopped in traffic or parked before using your car phone. It's particularly dangerous to dial while driving, so pre-program the numbers you call most often.

At the beginning of the conversation, let the person know you're on the car phone. That way if you start to fade in and out or are suddenly disconnected, the person will understand why.

Try to eliminate as much background noise as possible. Turn off the radio, roll up the windows, turn down the air conditioning. Then be sure to speak loudly and clearly.

Don't try to take notes while you're driving. Pull over or use a dictation device.

Before you call someone else's car phone, get permission. When someone is driving, a ringing phone can be a dangerous distraction. And, besides, incoming car phone calls are billed to the recipient.

*V*oice Mail

When you leave a voice mail message, you want to leave just as professional an impression as if you'd visited in person.

- Keep the message short.

- Speak slowly and enunciate.

- Give your name and phone number at the beginning of the message and at the end.

And, when you record a message on your own voice mail system to greet callers, be courteous and cheerful. Leave your callers with the updated information for reaching you elsewhere, or give them an idea of when you'll return their calls.

*B*eepers, Pagers, and Cellular Phones

Beepers, pagers, and cellular phones are annoying to others when activated in public places. Use them only if necessary. When responding to your cellular phone, go to a private place to talk.

9

Visitors

Whether you're hosting a visitor or you've been invited to visit someone else's office, you want to put your best foot forward from the first minute. If a visit begins on a sour note, you may well find yourself spending more of your time trying to repair the damage than tending to the real purpose of the visit.

Actually, the rules of business visiting etiquette are basically the same as those for social visiting.

For the host, it all boils down to gracious attention to your visitor's comfort. For the visitor, it requires consideration for the host's space and property. For both, it means respect for one another's time.

No matter what your position, status, or goal, chronic or unexplained lateness is never acceptable. It doesn't make you look more powerful or more important. Rather, it demonstrates a disregard for the other person's time or the fact that you're not professional enough to effectively manage your own time.

Handling Visitors in Your Office

Of course, even the best organized host may run a *few* minutes behind now and then. In that case, make sure your visitor is informed that the wait will be brief. Be certain the visitor has been offered comfortable seating, some reading material and, if possible, a beverage.

If you find that you will be unavoidably detained for a longer period, let your visitor know immediately. Give him or her the choice of waiting or rescheduling the visit. Apologize for the inconvenience.

Once the visitor has been shown into your office, offer him or her a seat. Come out from behind your desk to shake hands and greet your visitor. If possible, arrange the seating so you are sitting next to one another. Remember, a desk can be a daunting physical—and psychological—barrier to a guest. Even if there's no room in your office for side-by-side seating, at least place your chair directly beside your desk to remove that barrier.

As the host, it's your responsibility to initiate the conversation unless the visitor is the one who initiated the meeting. Some brief small talk about the weather, traffic, or some other general subject is usually sufficient to break the ice.

Make the visitor your first priority. Emergencies may arise from time to time, but interruptions for nonurgent phone calls or office "drop ins" shouldn't be permitted.

If you must take a phone call, keep it brief. If someone comes into your office with an urgent matter, introduce your guest.

Even after you've finished your business, the visit isn't over until your guest has left the premises. Walking your guest to the reception area is more than polite—it also eliminates the possibility that he or she will get lost. Before parting, shake hands and thank the guest for coming.

Visiting Others

"A funny thing happened to me on the way to our meeting…" Whatever your reason for being late, it had better be a good one. That's because most lateness can be avoided with a little pre-planning and organization.

First, when setting the date and time for a meeting, consider how that appointment fits into the rest of your day. Don't schedule back-to-back meetings at opposite ends of the city. Leave yourself some breathing room between appointments to allow for delays or other unforeseen problems.

If you're visiting someplace new or know that your destination is in a heavily traveled area, leave extra time in case you get lost or delayed by traffic jams.

For an early morning appointment, have all necessary materials ready to go the night before. Otherwise, do it first thing in the morning, before you become distracted by the demands of the workday.

Call your host if you find that you're going to be more than ten minutes late. Offer the option of rescheduling. When you arrive, apologize for the delay and the inconvenience.

Show respect for your host's space. Don't just grab the first available chair. Wait until the host indicates where you should sit. If he or she forgets, ask.

Don't move furniture without asking permission. And never put anything on your host's desk. Your purse or briefcase belong on the floor beside you.

Although the gracious host will minimize interruptions, he or she may have to take an urgent call or answer a co-worker's important question sometime during the course of your visit. In the case of the phone call, indicate through body language that you are willing to step outside to allow your host to speak in privacy. If someone else enters the room, stand.

Be sensitive to your host's body language and other clues to tell you when it's time to leave. If you need more time to conclude your business, give your host the option of scheduling a follow-up meeting.

When it's time to say "goodbye," shake hands and thank your host for his or her time. Follow up with a thank-you note, if appropriate.

10

Meetings and Presentations

Everytime you speak before a group, you communicate as much about yourself as about the topic at hand. Every communication opportunity is also a chance to demonstrate your professionalism, interpersonal skills, and effectiveness. On the other hand, poor communication skills can seriously undermine your image, even if you are the most technically proficient individual in the world.

Leading a Meeting

Did you know that people in middle management spend an average of 35 percent of the work week in meetings? And that for people in upper management, the average climbs to 50 percent?

Not all of these meetings are necessary, efficient, or productive. Before you decide to call a meeting, think about whether one is needed at all. Sometimes the same—or even better—results can be accomplished with a simple telephone call or letter.

If you conclude that a meeting is necessary after all, it's your responsibility to handle the planning. Planning is crucial not only if you hope to accomplish anything but also to show participants that you didn't call the meeting just to waste their time. So, in other words, planning is also a courtesy.

Follow the lead of journalists as you plan. Journalists have long used the "5 Ws and an H"—Who, What, When, Where, Why, and How—to ensure that they cover all the bases of a story. Put these elements in a slightly different order—Why, Who, Where, What, How, and When—and you'll cover all the bases for planning an effective meeting.

- **Why?** Determine the objective of your meeting. Decide what you hope to accomplish.

- **Who?** Invite only as many participants as necessary. If the objective of your meeting is to disseminate information or if it is a motivational meeting, the numbers can be larger than if the objective is to identify or solve a problem. A good guideline to follow is that the more interaction there will be, the fewer participants you should include.

- **Where?** Make the arrangements for the facilities. Choose a meeting space large enough to accommodate the number of participants, but not so large that vision and hearing are impaired. Arrange for any equipment and refreshments you will need.

- **What?** Plan an agenda detailing the topic areas and the order in which they'll be discussed. It's usually a good idea to discuss your agenda with the meeting participants prior to finalizing it. This way, you are less likely to be forced "off-track" by proposed changes and additions during the meeting itself. The agenda should be distributed to the participants two or three days in advance. Include any other materials that may be pertinent to the meeting.

  For long meetings, schedule short breaks every ninety minutes or so to allow people to stretch their legs and clear their heads. Keep the breaks to five to seven minutes. Any longer and you may have problems getting everyone reassembled and settled down.

- **How?** Develop some ground rules to make sure the meeting flows smoothly. Be firm about enforcing them. Rules should discourage interruptions, rude or disruptive behavior, and filibustering. They should encourage sharing of information, listening, and productive use of time.

- **When?** If possible, it's best to check with key participants before confirming the date. Give participants as much advance notice as possible so they can prepare materials and information to bring to the meeting.

There may be a number of people who don't need to attend the meeting but should still know that it will take place and what will be discussed. You can send these people an agenda with a note promising follow-up information after the meeting. This is also a good way to keep people in the loop who should attend the meeting but, for one reason or another, can't.

During the course of the meeting, it's your job as leader to facilitate. That means making sure the meeting begins and ends on time, stating the objectives, guiding the discussion so it follows the agenda, and enforcing the ground rules.

At the end of the meeting, it's also your job to review and clarify any actions that are to result from the meeting. Determine and verify who's accountable for what. Set deadlines with interim checkpoints.

After the other participants have left the meeting room, make sure you restore the room to its proper order. Return equipment. Pick up any trash.

Within forty-eight hours after the meeting, send out minutes. Minutes are simply a recap of what occurred at the meeting, including a list of objectives achieved, actions to be taken, the people who are accountable for those actions, any comments, and the date of a follow-up meeting, if appropriate.

*A*ttending a Meeting

When you're invited to attend a meeting, remember the "3 P's": punctuality, preparation, and participation.

- **Punctuality.** Get there on time. Whether you're meeting with one person or ten, making people wait is bad manners and bad for your image.

- **Preparation.** Ask the person planning the meeting what will be expected of you. What will be your role in the meeting? What materials or information should you bring?

- **Participation.** Present your materials and ideas. Keep your comments brief and to the point. Stick to the agenda. Listen with an open mind to what others have to say. Ask questions when you need to clarify something. Make notes on any follow-up actions you will be expected to take.

After the meeting, review the minutes and brief others in your department who should be aware of or involved in the results of the meeting and follow-up actions. Complete your action assignments on deadline.

*P*resentation Skills Etiquette

Being an effective speaker takes more than just knowing your topic. You can be the top authority in your field and still have trouble holding an audience's attention if you're not a courteous presenter.

You might wonder, what does courtesy have to do with a speaker's effectiveness—or lack of it? The answer is everything. Presentation courtesy means paying attention and responding to the interests and needs of your audience.

When planning a presentation, the first thing you should determine is exactly who your audience is. Why should they care what you have to say? What's in it for them?

Based on the answers to these questions, you can begin to prepare your presentation. Start with a one-sentence summary of your central theme. Then organize your information and support materials around that theme.

Make sure your language, materials, and conclusions are easy for your audience to follow and understand. You could be offering them the key to world peace, but if your audience is lost or asleep, they'll miss the point.

Include real-life examples to illustrate key points. This makes them easier to visualize and remember. If appropriate, inject some humor from time to time.

Be responsive to questions from the audience. Listen to the entire question before beginning your answer. If you don't think the entire audience has heard the question, repeat it. Keep your answer focused on the question—don't go off on tangents.

Manage your time. If you're scheduled to speak for twenty minutes, don't stretch it into a half hour. Overtime may be fine at sporting events, but at business presentations it only tends to make audiences fidgety. Practice your presentation to make sure you can fit everything you want to say into the allotted time.

11

Written Communication

Many people who are perfectly comfortable communicating their thoughts face to face or over the telephone freeze at the sight of paper and pen (or computer keyboard). Yet, even in this age of flip phones, car phones, and beepers, writing remains an essential skill for every business professional.

Writing does more than communicate ideas. It communicates importance. If you want to make something official, put it in writing. The written word also has permanence. Written records can provide documentation—a paper trail, if you will—to help you keep a permanent record of important information, transactions, or interactions.

General Writing Etiquette

You may be relieved to know that effective business writing is more a matter of good organization than of pure literary talent. Here are three basic guidelines to help you add clout to your next memo, letter, agenda, or thank-you note.

- **Ask yourself, "Should this communication be in writing?"** Just as important as knowing *how* to write is knowing *when* to write. Every company has its own protocol and guidelines. So be sure to know and follow yours.

  Think about whether a phone call or personal visit would be more appropriate in terms of time or company protocol. However, in most cases, it's best to write when you're expressing thanks; clarifying or confirming a phone conversation, plan of action, or agreement; or anytime the recipient is being asked to study a matter before coming to a conclusion or taking action.

- **Organize your thoughts.** Before you start to write, take a few minutes to think about the person you're writing to. Think about what you want to say and what you want the result of your written communication to be. A few minutes of organizational time up front can save a lot of rewriting time and aggravation.

Once you begin writing, get to the point as quickly as possible. Use the rest of your letter, memo, or whatever to support your central thought. If there are some things you want to particularly emphasize, underline or boldface them; just don't overdo it. Don't make the reader work to figure out what you're trying to say.

- **Be clear and concise.** Don't waste your reader's time or try his or her patience with unnecessary data or verbiage. Keep your language simple and your format brief. Eliminate extra words.

Thank-You Notes

If the last time you wrote a thank-you note was to thank your grandmother for a new bicycle she bought you when you were eight years old (and you only did it then because your mother made you), shame on you! Seriously, thank-you notes are more than good manners. They're good business.

A thank-you note can be an important public relations tool for the business professional. Not only does it demonstrate how gracious you are, it also shows that you value and appreciate other people.

A few well-chosen words of thanks can add a personal touch to a business relationship. At the same time, you're showing the recipient that you're a professional who follows up and pays attention to detail.

You already know that you should respond with a thank-you note when you receive a gift. But a written thank you is also appropriate on other occasions. Here are some of them:

- **Following a lunch or dinner with a new supplier or a visit to someone's home.** In this case, include the person's spouse, if appropriate.

- **To praise an employee or vendor for a job exceptionally well done.** In these cases, a verbal thank you may be nice, but a written thank you is much more substantial. A note can also be added to the recipient's personnel file.

- **Following a job interview or sales call.** Here, the thank-you note can do double duty. In addition to thanking the interviewee or prospect for his or her time, you should also restate your interest in the job or in serving the client or customer.

- **To thank your host after a business trip.** Be sure to send this as soon as possible after your return.

For maximum impact, you should send any thank-you note within twenty-four hours. Any longer and the recipient may wonder how appreciative you really are. Even worse, you may totally forget about your intention to write the note.

Because thank-you notes are more personal in nature than other forms of business communication, they should be handwritten if at all possible. One exception would be a note following a job interview—you can type these notes to make them appear more professional. And, oh yes, if your penmanship leaves something to be desired, type your notes to save your readers undue deciphering time and eyestrain. Just remember to sign your notes by hand.

Use good quality 5" x 7" or folded note paper. It should have your name and company name on it, but shouldn't look too formal. Stay away from stationery with cute pictures. It may be friendly, but it's not professional.

Make sure you know and use the recipient's correct name and title. Never guess on the spelling, even if the name seems common enough. There are many spelling variations on even the most common names.

Your closing should be appropriate—less than formal, but not overly familiar. Some good choices are "Sincerely" or "Best regards."

E-mail Courtesies

Just as all your other correspondence reflects your credibility and professionalism, e-mail messages convey an image of you too. You want it to be positive! Keep these tips in mind:

- Keep your message short.
- Don't use all capital letters. They scream at people.
- Pay attention to your spelling and grammar.
- And remember, e-mail really isn't private. Don't write anything you wouldn't want someone else to see!

12

Handling Criticism and Compliments Gracefully

Giving compliments and criticism must be handled with grace and tact in the business world. When giving compliments, you want to make sure they ring sincere. When offering feedback, you want to be assertive and make sure your point is understood, but without appearing defensive or confrontational. Likewise, when you're the recipient of a compliment or constructive feedback, you want to respond appropriately.

*G*iving Feedback

In business, it seems as if everyone's a critic—sometimes even you. And while taking or giving criticism is rarely viewed as a pleasant task, if handled correctly, it can actually boost your professional credibility and status.

The most important thing to remember is that criticism doesn't have to be negative or hurtful. On the contrary, it can and should be helpful if it is taken—and given—in the right manner.

Before offering your feedback to anyone, be sure that you have the authority and a solid reason to do so. Unsolicited feedback may provoke a negative or hostile response from the recipient. So, as always, think twice before you speak.

If, after careful consideration, you conclude that your feedback is both warranted and appropriate, remember that criticism can be a bitter pill for many people to swallow. Here are three tips for making your feedback as palatable—and valuable—as possible:

- Be tactful.
- Be specific.
- Be accurate.

Telling someone "You did a lousy job" doesn't accomplish anything besides making the person feel demoralized and defensive. You haven't really let the person know what he or she did wrong or offered suggestions for improvement. Typical responses to this type of criticism may be embarrassment, denial, or even outright hostility. It's best to take a positive and constructive approach to communicating your message. For example, you could say, "The estimates in this proposal should include a more comprehensive advertising budget."

No matter what the circumstances, insults, name-calling, and personal attacks are never warranted or acceptable. Focus on the behavior you want the person to change, not on the person. Avoid "you" statements such as "You really let me down." Keep in mind that in all probability, the person really wants to do the right thing. However, it's difficult for others to meet your expectations if they aren't certain of exactly what your expectations are.

If possible, mention some of the person's positive skills and contributions in your feedback. And be sure to offer specific suggestions for improvement. For example: "The research you did for this report is very thorough. In the future, however, please remember to use the spell-checker. There are four misspelled words."

Always wait for an appropriate time and choose a private location before offering criticism. No one appreciates being embarrassed in public, so don't choose the middle of a staff meeting or an encounter at the coffee machine, where your conversation is likely to be overheard by others.

After offering verbal criticism, it's often a good idea to follow up in writing. Today, many companies even require a written follow-up to ensure that the individual understands the key points and recommendations and to provide a record of the interaction.

*R*eceiving Feedback

If you find yourself on the receiving end of criticism—and everyone does from time to time—the most important thing to remember is to remain calm and to fight the natural instinct to become defensive or paranoid. The following five tips can help you handle criticism in stride and, better yet, turn it into a positive learning experience.

- **Listen.** Don't start arguing or making excuses. Everybody makes mistakes or could use improvement in some areas. Keep an open mind.

- **Consider the source.** Does the speaker have the authority, knowledge, and expertise to give you this feedback? Does he or she have an ulterior motive? (Be careful not to invent one just to make yourself feel better.)

- **Ask for examples.** Don't accept generalities such as "poor," "disappointing," or "lousy." Ask the speaker to tell you exactly what is wrong. Using phrases such as "What exactly was wrong with the presentation?" or "Help me to understand what you mean by 'poor'" can help you get more information.

- **Evaluate the criticism.** If it's valid, accept it gracefully and with a positive attitude. Tell the speaker you appreciate his or her comments and be enthusiastic about your willingness and ability to use them to improve your performance.

- **Keep the useful information, but let go of the negative feelings.** Don't dwell on the embarrassment of being criticized. Hold your head up high and move on.

*G*iving Compliments

Everybody needs to feel appreciated. A word of praise can do wonders for the spirit—and the motivation—of any employee.

You don't have to gush over someone to express your appreciation. A simple "Good job—keep up the good work" is enough to make most people feel good. The amount and specific wording of your praise should suit your personality. Low-key is fine as long as it's sincere.

Some people hesitate to compliment employees because they are afraid the praise might "go to their heads." To avoid that possibility, be specific and focus your praise on the particular action or accomplishment rather than on the person in general. You might, for example, say, "The way you organized that report made it very easy for the client to read and understand."

Increase the impact of your praise by giving it in writing or, at least, in public, whenever possible and appropriate. Also, remember to put a copy of any complimentary notes or memos in your employee's permanent personnel file.

If you have something nice to say, don't wait. Do it right away before you forget. Besides, according to the principles of behavior modification, the sooner you reinforce positive behavior, the more likely it is to be repeated.

*R*eceiving Compliments

A little humility is a good thing. But too much can be as detrimental to your image as too little.

It's not arrogant or immodest to accept a compliment. As long as you do it gracefully. In fact, false modesty is more than unbecoming. It can be downright insulting to the person who paid you the compliment in the first place.

"Thank you" is always a polite and correct way to acknowledge a compliment. Don't add, "It was nothing" or some other qualifying statement that diminishes you and your accomplishment. However, it's perfectly appropriate to acknowledge others who may have been instrumental in your success ("I couldn't have done it without Sally and Ted") or something valuable you may have learned from the experience.

13

Giving and Accepting Gifts

In some cultures, gift-giving rituals are a central part of doing business. In the United States, the giving of business gifts is governed more by the particular culture and customs of each company.

The right gift can speak volumes about your esteem for the recipient. So can the wrong one. Therefore, it's important to think carefully about the company policy and tradition, circumstances, recipient, cost of the gift, and nature of the gift before giving.

- **Company policy and tradition.** Some companies have definite rules governing the giving and receiving of gifts. For instance, some companies may view the giving of gifts by a vendor to be a form of bribery. Some set dollar limits on the value of gifts that employees may receive. In other companies, gift-giving parameters are governed more by tradition. Either way, it's important that you know what is—and isn't—appropriate for the recipient's company before you present a gift.

- **The circumstances.** A gift can help you express gratitude, congratulations, sympathy, and holiday wishes. Likewise, it can acknowledge personal or professional milestones (e.g., fiftieth birthday, retirement). Again, consider the company's gift-giving policy and tradition before you give.

- **The recipient.** Are you close personal friends with the recipient or simply business acquaintances? Is the recipient your boss, a client or customer, or your secretary? Your relationship with the person should be a major determining factor in your gift selection. The most appreciated gifts are the ones that are selected specifically for the recipient, with his or her particular taste or individual interests in mind.

- **The cost.** This can be a sticky one. You don't want to be seen as cheap, but you also don't want to be overly extravagant. Again, look to company policy or tradition for guidance. And always keep in mind that quality doesn't have to be exorbitantly costly.

- **The nature of the gift.** No matter how well you know the recipient or how good a sense of humor he or she has, tacky, suggestive, or romantic gifts are never appropriate in a business setting. If in doubt, a gift of some favorite food is usually welcome. You can also always fall back on the traditional "professional" gifts such as pocket calendars and books.

If you are the recipient of a gift, be gracious. Even if you thank the giver in person, follow up with a note. Include a specific positive statement about the gift. For example: "Thank you for your thoughtful gift. The pen is so beautiful that I keep it displayed on my desk."

There may come a time when you receive a gift that, for one reason or another, is inappropriate and must be returned. If the sender was obviously well-intentioned, be gracious and gentle and offer a plausible explanation. For example, if the cost of the gift exceeded the parameters set by your company, you might say, "It was very nice of you to think of me, but company policy will not allow me to accept this gift."

If a gift is obviously inappropriate or offensive, your refusal can still be tactful and, at the same time, assertive: "The gift you sent to me is inappropriate. I am returning it to you." Keep a copy of the note and a record of how you returned the gift (e.g., a postal receipt, etc.) in your files.

14

Business Travel

Whether you travel frequently for your job or just occasionally, when you're "on the road," you can expect the unexpected. And it's often in these unplanned moments that your business etiquette and professionalism get a mighty workout.

Whatever the purpose of your business trip, there are two major keys to success: preparation and flexibility. These two things may seem incompatible, but they're

93

really not. In fact, they're the equally important complementary sides of the professional personality. Just remember that good manners don't belong only in your home office.

Travel Tips

Preparing for your trip begins with focusing on its purpose. Perhaps you are traveling to visit a client or customer or a prospect. Or you may be a participant in contract negotiations. You may be a presenter at a conference or an attendee. Or you may be a trouble-shooter or district manager whose job requires you to cover extensive geographical territories.

Whatever your purpose, careful scheduling is crucial. That means more than booking your airline tickets, hotel reservations, and car rentals. It means planning a comprehensive itinerary—and writing it down. Your itinerary should include dates and phone numbers of where you'll be as well as any meetings you have scheduled. You should make three copies of your itinerary—one for you, one to leave at the office for your secretary or other co-worker, and one for your family. Doing this is not only courteous, it's also a necessity if you must be reached in an emergency.

Contact anyone you need to see during your trip to coordinate schedules. If you don't, you risk flying all the way across the country only to find that the person you need to see is on vacation! Or much to your embarassment, you may force your contact into making last-minute schedule changes to accommodate you.

Prepare any documents or other materials you need to bring along. Don't wait until the last minute. Being thousands of miles from the office and realizing that you've forgotten a key part of your presentation can be devastating.

Choose your travel wardrobe with your itinerary in mind. Will you be attending a gala formal dinner, or a golf tournament? Pack accordingly. Remember that even if the dress code is "casual," that means *business* casual—comfortable, yet always professional.

Pack as light as possible. Mix-and-match wardrobe pieces offer maximum versatility while taking up a minimum of space in your suitcase. Wrinkle-resistant fabrics that don't show soil are your best choices.

Consider whether business gifts are appropriate. In some cultures, they may even be expected. Find out before you go.

So, now you know how to prepare for your business trip. But what happens if, despite all your careful preparation, something goes awry? Perhaps you miss your connecting flight, or you land in Cleveland while your luggage travels on to San Diego or, well, you get the idea.

That's where flexibility comes in. No matter what happens, the first thing to do is take a deep breath. Every problem has a solution. However, if you're jumping up and down and hyperventilating, you're in no condition to figure one out.

A little clear thinking and a good sense of humor can help you get through just about anything. Often, the way you handle a crisis can tell people more about your professionalism than they would have learned had everything gone according to plan.

*T*ravel Etiquette

You're confined in a limited space with a crowd of strangers for an extended period of time. The seating is elbow-to-elbow. Just about everyone, including you, is tired and, at least to some degree, frazzled. Every move you make has an effect on someone else and vice versa.

Travel can be a most grueling test of manners. In the close quarters of an airplane or train, every inch of space can become fiercely coveted territory. Be conscious of what space belongs to you—and what space doesn't. Don't stretch out into the aisle or sprawl into your neighbor's seat. Don't kick the seat in front of you.

Keep your belongings within the confines of your own space. Airline regulations require you to stow carry-on luggage in overhead compartments or under your seat. Certainly the primary reason for this is safety. But it is also the polite thing to do. If your luggage doesn't fit in either of these two designated places, have it checked in for storage with the rest of the luggage.

Ask your neighbor's permission before adjusting air, light, or window shades. Your comfort may be another person's misery.

Small talk between passengers is often appropriate and even welcome, especially during long trips. However, your neighbor may prefer to read, sleep, work, or simply be left alone. If the person is not responsive, don't push it. Find something else to do or someone else to talk to.

When traveling, be sensitive to the special needs of other people. For example, if someone has a disability, be patient if that person takes a few minutes longer to get settled in his or her seat.

Whether you're in a hurry or not, pushing and shoving is rude. Besides, it won't get you where you're going any faster. So, whether you're boarding, disembarking, or getting your luggage, wait your turn.

Traveling in a taxi can present a set of etiquette challenges all its own. In many major cities, simply getting a taxi is a feat of survival. Everyone is in a hurry and everyone has important business—just like you.

If you're staying at or visiting a hotel, let the doorman or other designated staff member hail a cab for you. It's not only proper etiquette to allow the person to do his or her job, it's usually the most practical and quickest way to get a cab. Remember to tip the doorman one to two dollars—depending on the difficulty the person had hailing the cab.

When two people are waiting in the same location to catch a cab, the general guideline is first come, first served—regardless of gender. However, either party can graciously yield, particularly if one has a pressing engagement and the other doesn't. In some cities, people also have the option of sharing a cab and its costs, even if they're going to different destinations.

It can be irritating while you're stuck in a traffic jam to watch the fare on the meter go higher and higher even though you aren't moving. However, it's not fair to ask the driver to turn off the meter. In most cases, drivers are reimbursed partly for their time as well as mileage.

Along with the required fare, include an appropriate tip. Fifteen percent of the total fare is standard.

*T*raveling With Your Spouse or Significant Other

Traveling with your spouse or significant other can make a business trip seem more like a holiday. However, you and your partner must always keep in mind that the first priority of the trip is business.

Time together for touring or enjoying other activities must be scheduled around business—not vice versa. Your partner must also be flexible enough to gracefully accept a sudden change in plans.

When you are attending business functions together, your partner should dress appropriately and be prepared to mingle with your bosses, clients or customers, co-workers, and their spouses or significant others. Above all, there should be no griping about long meetings and jam-packed business schedules—just patience, politeness, and a positive attitude.

15

Coping With Conflict

Conflict is never pleasant, but it's something you can't totally avoid, no matter how hard you try. In fact, sometimes trying too hard to avoid conflict can allow a disagreement that might have been settled with a few well-chosen words to escalate into all-out war!

The trick is to deal with conflict *before* it gets out of hand. Of course, that doesn't mean nitpicking everything everyone says or does. It simply means identifying real areas of disagreement and trying to resolve them in a calm, rational, and civil manner.

Whenever two people don't agree on how to handle a particular situation, the potential for conflict exists—whether it's a dispute over office space, work distribution, or status. Whatever the source of potential conflict, the best way to handle it is to:

- **Think before you speak.** Focus on the specific behavior or situation that's at the root of the problem. Generalizations and personal attacks don't solve anything. They only create more conflict and, in the end, nobody wins.

- **Ask yourself, "Is it worth it?"** Some things such as a desk or parking space may not be worth arguing over. Choose your fights carefully. You don't want to be viewed as overbearing or petty. Besides, a gracious concession every once in a while can show people how reasonable and professional you can be.

- **Go straight to the source.** Nobody likes a tattletale. Besides, a sign of the true professional is being able to solve your own problems rather than running to the boss with every little thing.

  Make sure that you approach the person in private. And try to arrange for a meeting on neutral ground—somewhere other than your office or the other person's.

- **Hold your temper.** Don't let anger get the better of you. Don't accuse the person with "you" statements or resort to name-calling.

Assertiveness and aggressiveness are two different things. Assertiveness is strong and professional; aggressiveness is overbearing and threatening. For example, if someone brings up a topic you don't want to discuss right then, you should say so—but in an assertive, not a nasty or aggressive way. A simple, "I'm not comfortable discussing this topic now and would like to postpone discussion until our next meeting" stated calmly should be enough to get the message across loud and clear.

Pay attention to the pitch and volume of your voice. Keep them both calm and steady. Also watch your body language. No crossed arms or finger-pointing. Maintain eye contact.

- **Keep an open mind.** Listen to the other person's side of the story. Sometimes knowing the motivation behind a particular behavior can give you a clue to a fair and mutually acceptable solution.

- **Stay focused.** If there are a number of issues involved, address each one separately. Don't lump them all into one single "You're out to get me" issue.

- **Be flexible.** Try to work out solutions together. Make your suggestions, and then listen to the other person's. When you come to a conclusion on an issue, restate it to confirm agreement.

- **Follow through.** Be prepared to stick to your end of the agreement. If the other person doesn't, offer a polite reminder. If necessary, put it in writing.

- **If all else fails.** If you really can't come to a mutually acceptable conclusion, you should consider taking the problem to a higher authority within the company. This should be done only if the matter is truly important and if all other attempts at working it out between you have failed.

It's important to add that no one should be expected to put up with off-color, sexist, racist, or otherwise offensive comments or behavior. Don't apologize or explain. A simply stated, "I'm offended by that" should get your point across.

*T*ake Stock of Yourself

Sometimes we're so busy watching everyone else's manners that we fail to recognize our own shortcomings. To avoid becoming the source of conflict, make sure you think before you speak and show some sensitivity to the people and situations around you.

Do you refer to women as "girls" or a particular ethnic or religious group as "you people"? Make sure you know the correct terms of address to avoid insulting or otherwise offending anyone.

Do you lump everyone of a particular gender or ethnic group or religious affiliation into a single category with shared characteristics and behaviors? For instance, if a woman is having a bad day, do you automatically assume that her hormones are the cause? Don't. Every person is an individual and should be treated as one.

Do you believe that the only correct viewpoint on any topic is the one you hold? There's nothing more irritating than a know-it-all. Learn to listen and respect other people's points of view. Who knows? You just might learn something!

16

International Etiquette

Today's workplace spans the entire globe, encompassing countries and cultures that many of us have never encountered before. This globalization of business has literally opened up whole new worlds of opportunity for American professionals. At the same time, it has presented a whole new dimension of etiquette challenges.

While the need for politeness and respect is universal, the way they are communicated is not. Each culture has its own rules, traditions, and protocols. What is appropriate and polite in one culture may be totally inappropriate and even offensive in another.

Business professionals can't afford to make etiquette mistakes—either at home or abroad. Even if your faux pas is nothing more than an honest error, the cost in damaged relationships and lost business can be terribly high. And with the availability of cross-cultural reference materials and training programs today, "I didn't know" is no longer an acceptable excuse.

When You're the Guest

You've no doubt heard the saying, "When in Rome, do as the Romans do." For the international business traveler, this is one of the keys to success.

Whatever your purpose in visiting another country, your first job is to adapt. Before you leave home, do some research. Go to the library. Talk to people from the country you're planning to visit. If possible, become familiar with the food of the country by visiting restaurants in the U.S. that specialize in its cuisine. Some basics that you should know are appropriate greetings, gift-giving rituals, currency, as much of the language as possible, and any religious beliefs and customs that are integral to the culture.

Once you arrive, carefully observe the behaviors of the people who live in the country. Don't be afraid to ask questions; it shows an open mind, a willingness to learn, and a desire to be respectful. In many circumstances, find a mentor or guide to show you the lay of the land—both geographically and culturally.

During your stay, try to make an effort to look at things from the perspective of the host culture—not from your own. That means not judging or criticizing other people's manners because they don't fit American standards. Remember, your hosts may be working very hard not to judge or criticize *your* manners.

Be open to new things. Have a sense of adventure. Try the local cuisine. Use every new experience to broaden your knowledge and your horizons.

When You're the Host

Although it's the visitor's job to adapt to the local culture, it's the duty of the gracious host to make it as easy and comfortable as possible for the visitor to do so. As the host, you should make the effort to learn all you can about the visitor's culture prior to the visit. That way, you will be better able to view your own culture through your visitor's eyes and anticipate many of the questions or problems he or she may have.

Your guest should feel welcome from the moment of arrival. You or someone you designate should be waiting at the airport to greet your visitor when the plane lands. Be certain that you—or the person you designate—understands and uses appropriate greeting protocol. It's a sign of respect for the visitor and the culture that he or she represents. Again, if you don't know what constitutes an acceptable greeting in your guest's culture, find out.

Arrange for a delivery of food or flowers to the visitor's hotel room. This gesture is particularly meaningful if the gift selection is based on a knowledge of the person's culture, customs, and individual taste.

Invite the visitor to your home. In addition to providing a glimpse of American home life, this gesture can help to establish a bond between you and your guest.

Whether you are dining with your guest at your home or in a restaurant, be sensitive to the visitor's dining customs, restrictions, and preferences. Never try to force a guest to try your favorite American delicacy. Some cultures have very strict dietary laws. Or your guest simply may have a personal reason for refusing.

If it's the visitor's first trip, offer to conduct a personal tour of your city. Arrange for a driver and transportation to be available during your guest's stay, so that he or she may feel free to sightsee or enjoy other activities in safety and comfort. Provide maps and materials about the city's points of interests.

Evenings can be especially lonely for someone far from home. Unless your visitor prefers to spend those after-work hours alone, plan some interesting evening entertainment that you think he or she might enjoy. Unless you know your visitor's preferences well, offer a choice of options—an evening at the theater, a baseball game, or a concert, for example. If the guest is accompanied by his or her family, plan activities everyone can enjoy.

17

Business Associates With Special Needs

Until recently, many workplaces were simply not equipped to meet the special needs of physically challenged employees. However, since the passage of the Americans With Disabilities Act (ADA) in 1992, businesses have been required by law to make every reasonable effort to create environments in which individuals with disabilities can function as productive members of the workforce.

With the widening of doorways, the installation of ramps, the construction of accessible restroom facilities, and other necessary accommodations, many physically challenged workers are now able to function more easily and effectively in the work environment. But, in many instances, one barrier still remains.

Many people who aren't physically challenged are nervous or uncomfortable around people who are. In most cases, it's not a matter of rudeness. Quite the opposite. Many people *fear* they will offend the other person because they don't quite know the right things to say or do.

There's only one rule to remember when dealing with a physically challenged person: Put the emphasis on the *person* and not on the disability.

No one likes to feel ignored and isolated. Yet, many times, people with seeing or hearing challenges are made to feel invisible. Never assume that because a person has a disability, he or she can't or doesn't want to communicate.

When you would like to initiate a conversation with a hearing impaired person, place yourself within easy sight of the person, wave, or gently tap the person on the shoulder. If the person is reading your lips, be sure to speak slowly and form your words clearly. Stay within the person's most comfortable line of vision.

Speak directly to hearing impaired people. Maintain eye contact directly with them, not with the interpreter. Don't use third-person references. Instead of asking the interpreter "Would she like a cup of coffee?" ask the person directly—"Would *you* like a cup of coffee?"

When approaching a person with a visual impairment, identify yourself immediately. Take care not to startle the person with your sudden presence.

When conversing with someone who has difficulty speaking, be patient and attentive. Listen carefully. Don't interrupt. If you don't understand, let the person know. Repeat the part you do understand and let the person continue.

Don't assume that because a person is in a wheelchair or motorized cart that he or she cannot hear, see, or speak. To make conversation easier and more natural, try to get on that person's eye level.

When being introduced to a person with a disability, be prepared to shake hands. Be conscious of which hand the person offers. A person who has an artificial limb may offer a left hand instead of the traditional right. Respond in kind. If the person is blind, ask, "Shall we shake hands?" and then touch your hand to his or hers.

Never pet or interact with a person's guide dog without asking permission. The dog may become agitated or otherwise distracted from its work.

Don't refer to the person as a "victim" of his or her disability or call someone a "blind person." Most people with physical challenges resent being defined by their disabilities; therefore, be sensitive and neutral in your descriptions. Instead of "handicap," use disability. Instead of "blind person," use "person with a visual impairment."

Finally, if you are not sure whether to offer assistance to a physically challenged person, ask first. If the person needs help, he or she will provide you with instructions. If the answer is no, respect the refusal. Don't push the issue.

Available From SkillPath Publications

Self-Study Sourcebooks

Climbing the Corporate Ladder: What You Need to Know and Do to Be a Promotable Person *by Barbara Pachter and Marjorie Brody*

Coping With Supervisory Nightmares: 12 Common Nightmares of Leadership and What You Can Do About Them *by Michael and Deborah Singer Dobson*

Defeating Procrastination: 52 Fail-Safe Tips for Keeping Time on Your Side *by Marlene Caroselli, Ed.D.*

Discovering Your Purpose *by Ivy Haley*

Going for the Gold: Winning the Gold Medal for Financial Independence *by Lesley D. Bissett, CFP*

Having Something to Say When You Have to Say Something: The Art of Organizing Your Presentation *by Randy Horn*

Info-Flood: How to Swim in a Sea of Information Without Going Under *by Marlene Caroselli, Ed.D.*

The Innovative Secretary *by Marlene Caroselli, Ed.D.*

Letters & Memos: Just Like That! *by Dave Davies*

Mastering the Art of Communication: Your Keys to Developing a More Effective Personal Style *by Michelle Fairfield Poley*

Organized for Success! 95 Tips for Taking Control of Your Time, Your Space, and Your Life *by Nanci McGraw*

A Passion to Lead! How to Develop Your Natural Leadership Ability *by Michael Plumstead*

P.E.R.S.U.A.D.E.: Communication Strategies That Move People to Action *by Marlene Caroselli, Ed.D.*

Productivity Power: 250 Great Ideas for Being More Productive *by Jim Temme*

Promoting Yourself: 50 Ways to Increase Your Prestige, Power, and Paycheck *by Marlene Caroselli, Ed.D.*

Proof Positive: How to Find Errors Before They Embarrass You *by Karen L. Anderson*

Risk-Taking: 50 Ways to Turn Risks Into Rewards *by Marlene Caroselli, Ed.D. and David Harris*

Speak Up and Stand Out: How to Make Effective Presentations *by Nanci McGraw*

Stress Control: How You Can Find Relief From Life's Daily Stress *by Steve Bell*

The Technical Writer's Guide *by Robert McGraw*

Total Quality Customer Service: How to Make It Your Way of Life *by Jim Temme*

Write It Right! A Guide for Clear and Correct Writing *by Richard Andersen and Helene Hinis*

Your Total Communication Image *by Janet Signe Olson, Ph.D.*

andbooks

Notes